I WANT TO BE A
METEOROLOGIST

Written by
Jonathan Reule

Illustration
Maria Fernanda De Oliveira Sevaroli

Storyboard
Keziah Gan

UNIBINO
B O O K S

First paperback edition October 2023
ISBN 978-981-17320-5-8

Published by Unibino Pte. Ltd.
9 North Buona Vista Drive, #02-01 Metropolis Tower 1, Singapore 138588

www.unibino.com

Weather can have a great impact on our daily lives. It affects almost everything around us, from the clothes we wear to the buildings we live in and the plans we make for the coming days. This is why knowing and understanding the weather is so important in our modern world, and nobody understands this better than meteorologists.

You see, Meteorologists are trained scientists who use special instruments and computer programs to gather data about temperature, air pressure, humidity, wind, clouds, and precipitation.

From there, they can make predictions about upcoming events and give warnings, especially when dangerous atmospheric events are on the horizon. So, if you like science and the idea of studying the natural weather patterns in our world, then perhaps being a meteorologist might be the right path for you!

Before we get caught up in this whirlwind of excitement, it's good to take a step back and uncover how this career formed into a modern profession. And to get that answer, we need to travel all the way back to prehistoric times. You see, humans have always had a special relationship with the world we inhabit.

Since the beginning of humanity, we have strived to take care of ourselves and adapt to the natural environment around us. However, this has not always been a simple feat. Even though we may reside in sturdy homes and travel around in metal-clad vehicles now, it hasn't always been this way. Back in the long-ago past, our buildings were made from more flimsy materials, and our mode of transportation was often our own two feet.

This type of living made us extremely exposed to the unpredictable nature of our environment. Thunderstorms could easily cause the collapse of our homes, leaving us without shelter. Abrupt snowstorms could wipe out our food sources and put our lives at risk. We had to be constantly vigilant and prepare ourselves for whatever nature could throw our way.

In order to survive in such a harsh environment, people had to become adept at reading the signs of the natural world. They learned how to predict when a storm was coming, how to prepare for it, and how to avoid possible dangers brought on by erratic weather. But as our societies grew more complex, so too did our need for accurate weather forecasting.

Soon, people sought to explain the various phenomena they observed in the world around them. Many ancient civilisations attributed weather patterns to astrology or the actions of powerful deities. The ancient Greeks believed that atmospheric activity was caused by divine beings residing in the sky.

To try and appease these gods, they even developed rain-making dance rituals. However, when this didn't work out, the excuse was often that either the dance was done wrongly or the gods were not happy with the performance. Despite their beliefs, these ancient societies were far from understanding the true causes of weather.

Although, not everyone was convinced that the gods were to blame for weather patterns. In fact, one man from Greece, Aristotle, hypothesised that the weather was a result of the four fundamental elements - fire, air, water, and wind - which he believed constituted all matter and phenomena on Earth.

Aristotle is widely regarded as the first official meteorologist. He authored an essay titled Μετεωρολογικά, which translates to Meteorology in English. Based on his observations of the natural world, he hypothesised that thunderstorms were a result of water vapour being evaporated into the atmosphere and subsequently sent back down to earth by winds blowing through the clouds. Although some of his theories required refinement, several of them were still excellent building blocks and remain precise by modern meteorological standards.

Unfortunately, not everyone was willing to accept Aristotle's theories during his time, and many continued to cling to their traditional notions about the causes of weather. Furthermore, the absence of technology made it difficult to prove Aristotle's theories. But in time, people from other nations started to take note of Aristotle's work and even helped to expand upon its understanding.

During the 2nd Century AD, Ptolemy, a Roman mathematician, authored the book called Almagest, which focused primarily on astronomy but incorporated numerous insights from Aristotle's prior work on meteorology. Ptolemy's work included weather forecasts regarding cloud formation and distinguished the world into distinct climate zones, recognising that weather conditions would differ across various regions. To Ptolemy, it was expected that lands closer to the equator would experience warmer weather, while those in the artic regions would often remain below freezing.

Fortunately, we persisted in constructing and inventing devices that could facilitate scientific research. However, most of the early meteorological instruments invented were used by farmers or governments to better track their crop productions or anticipate any unfavourable weather on its way. For example, in Korea's Joseon dynasty, Prince Munjong created an official rain gauge and distributed them to farms nationwide, enabling more precise taxation of citizens based on their harvests.

Around the same period, another significant invention was made by the architect Leon Battista Alberti - the anemometer. This device was used to measure the wind's speed, direction, and velocity with exceptional precision.

Even though others introduced some variations of the device, Alberti's anemometer was so well-designed that it became the standard measurement tool for centuries to come.

As instruments to measure the Earth's atmosphere were developed, our scientific understanding of weather increased. Among these devices were the thermometer, barometer, and hygrometer. With these new tools, we could make more accurate hypothesis about the atmosphere, leading to better short-term predictions about upcoming weather events.

The barometer was particularly useful in measuring atmospheric pressure, which can indicate sudden changes in weather, especially when storms are brewing nearby. The thermometer allowed us to measure temperatures, enabling us to record sudden spikes in temperature - another warning sign of impending weather events such as heat waves or snowstorms.

Meanwhile, the hygrometer measures water density in an area, providing a way to gauge current humidity in the surrounding region.

The 1900s marked a turning point in the history of weather forecasting as scientists began to explore more advanced methods for predicting weather patterns. In 1904, Norwegian scientist Vilhelm Bjerknes proposed that short-term changes in weather could be predicted using mathematical calculations. He was resolute that with precise measurement tools, forecasting the weather could become a straightforward task.

Despite being introduced in the early 1900s, numerical weather prediction only gained widespread acceptance in the 1920s with the emergence of a better understanding of atmospheric physics. But it was not until the 1950s, with the advent of faster and more efficient computers, that meteorologists were able to process large amounts of data and produce more accurate weather forecasts than ever before.

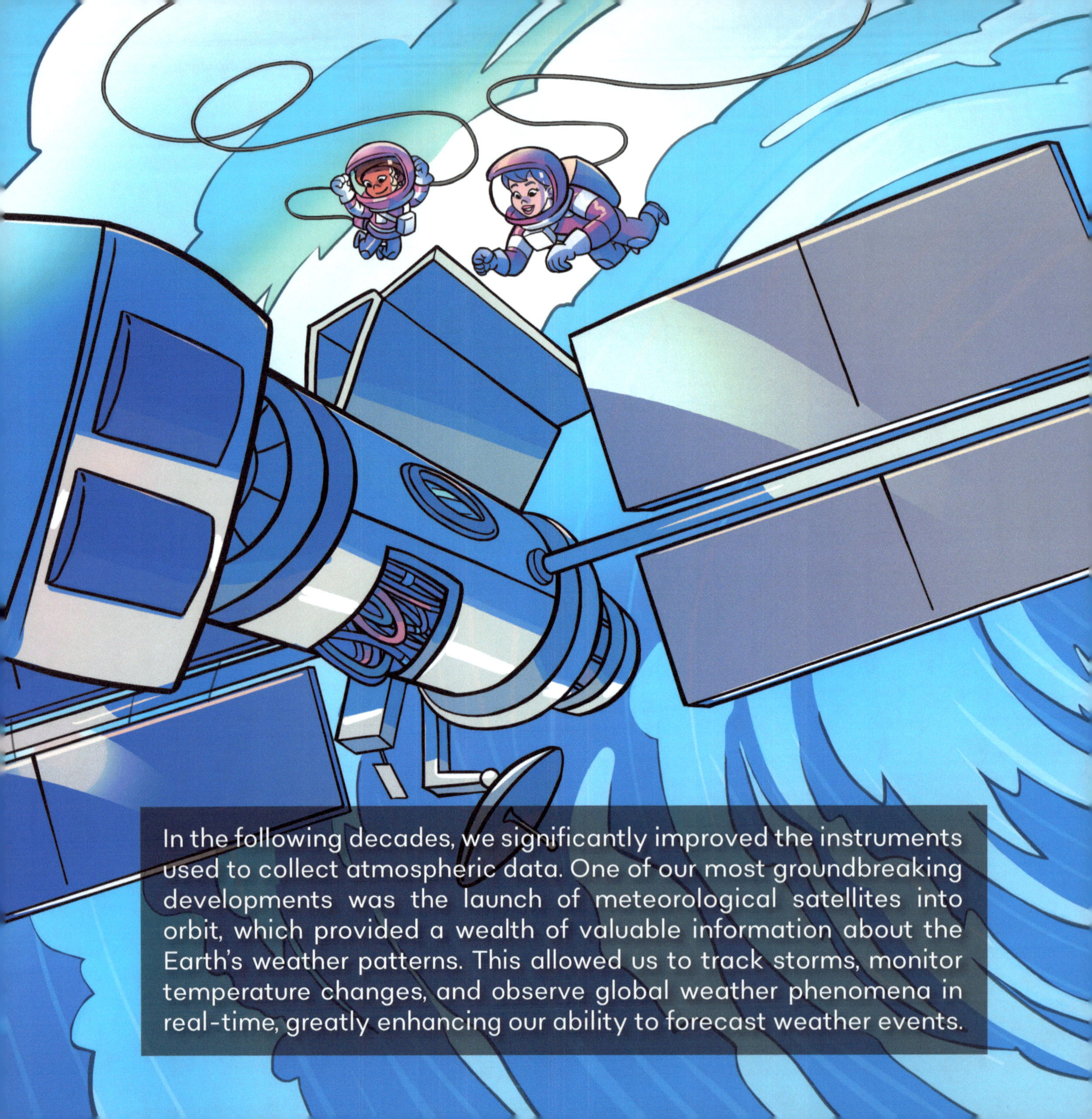

In the following decades, we significantly improved the instruments used to collect atmospheric data. One of our most groundbreaking developments was the launch of meteorological satellites into orbit, which provided a wealth of valuable information about the Earth's weather patterns. This allowed us to track storms, monitor temperature changes, and observe global weather phenomena in real-time, greatly enhancing our ability to forecast weather events.

Satellites continue to play a critical role in providing up-to-date information on weather patterns. These technological advancements have revolutionised our ability to not only monitor daily weather conditions but also forecast dangerous natural phenomena such as hurricanes, blizzards, sandstorms, and even tornadoes.

By utilising this invaluable data, we can send out warnings and evacuation notices to those in the path of these impending disasters, ultimately saving countless lives.

Now, learning about this information may have you wondering what the role of a meteorologist entails and what steps are necessary to pursue this stormy profession. Typically, those who choose this profession possess a keen interest in earth sciences and the examination of weather patterns. As such, they often enrol in a specialised program at the college level, specifically focused on meteorology or atmospheric sciences. Those who are particularly passionate about the field may even choose to pursue a master's degree or even a PhD in this area of study.

After that, aspiring meteorologists will then take their learnings and apply them in the real world. This often requires them to be savvy with technology, such as computer software and other devices used to gather atmospheric data. Meteorologists also need to be good at maths and ready to work with tricky calculations when compiling all their findings.

First, we have Atmospheric Physicists who dedicate their time to studying the physical movements that occur in the atmosphere. Along with that, they also see how different terrains, such as mountains or flatlands, can influence a change in weather.

Whereas Operational Meteorologists are tasked with the responsibility of generating weather forecasts for institutions requiring up-to-date weather reports.

Operational Meteorologists can be found working in various places, but their job duties are often the same, to collect data and give accurate interpretations about upcoming weather patterns. You may find them working for national weather institutions, weather stations, or even military bases!

Another great career is in meteorological tech development. This field focuses on making new technologies or enhancing already established equipment to more accurately perceive weather-related elements. In this career, meteorologists will need to consult on the development of these technologies and offer guidance on how best to construct them so that they can be enhanced.

While Broadcast meteorologists focus on presenting weather forecasts, either on television or radio. They don't normally work on generating predictions like operational meteorologists but rather take those findings and relay the information in concise terms to the general public. For these meteorologists, it's important not only to have a strong foundation in weather sciences but also an extroverted personality, or at least be ready to speak in front of the camera on a regular basis.

In addition, Forensic meteorologists may be called upon to provide expert testimony in court cases, particularly in situations where unusual weather events have occurred. For instance, they might testify about the dryness of an area where a fire was started or the iciness of the road where a car accident happened.
These meteorologists are particularly helpful when someone may be wrongly accused of an incident caused by an act of nature.

However, there are some meteorologists who choose to concentrate their energies on researching more about weather conditions. They may take a position at a university as a research professor or at a larger weather institute like the NOAA. They may also narrow their study to one aspect of weather, such as studying tornadoes or snowstorms.

Whether you dream of becoming a broadcast meteorologist, predicting weather patterns, or being a research scientist, the world of meteorology is full of possibilities. As a meteorologist, you'll have the chance to use your knowledge and expertise to make a real impact on people's lives.

As long as we live on this planet, we will always need meteorologists to help us understand and prepare for the ever-changing weather conditions that impact our lives. From the farmers who rely on accurate weather forecasts to plan their harvests to the pilots who need real-time information about weather patterns to ensure safe flights, meteorologists play a crucial role in society. So if you have a passion for the weather and a desire to make a difference, consider a career in meteorology. With hard work and dedication, you can build a rewarding career in a field that offers endless possibilities for growth and exploration.

My Inspiration

Shubhi Saxena
Founder, Unibino

As a parent in this ever-changing world, it can sometimes feel overwhelming when it comes to our children's futures. New technologies seem to be arising almost every day, and with so many innovations, it creates unique professions which many of us wouldn't have dreamed to be necessary only a few years ago. Which to me is a good thing. Because with so much variety, my children can have the opportunity to pick a career that will fit their personalities and build upon their strengths. As you may imagine, this desire within me to provide my children with the resources they needed to thrive, led me to search out books that would be easy enough for them to understand while teaching them about various professions.

Only, I found that these books were few and far between. Even if I could find a book about a certain profession geared towards young readers, I found them sparse inside and limited to only certain careers that may not fit my children's abilities. This is when I came up with the idea to write my own children's books, teaching them about all the various careers in the modern world. After months of researching different professions and learning more than I ever expected, I quickly realised this was going to be a bigger project than I first anticipated. I dove into the histories of these professions, discovering links to the past, and why these professions were now so important.

Ultimately my goal was to offer my children options, to show them that there is no one set path for everyone. But in this, I stumbled upon something bigger. I wanted to share this with future generations. To share with all children and parents about these careers, to help spark curiosity, and to instil a passion for the future. Everyone has special talents and abilities, and I hope that this series will be able to offer clarity and inspiration to children around the world. Because at the end of the day, it's never too early to start dreaming and never too late to take action. With this, I hope you enjoy this series and that your young ones become the best versions of themselves as they can achieve.